James Aitchison

Learning How to Sing

Learning How to Sing
published in the United Kingdom in 2018
by Mica Press

c/o Leslie Bell 47 Belle Vue Road, Wivenhoe,
Colchester, Essex CO7 9LD
www.micapress.co.uk | books@micapress.co.uk

ISBN 978-1-869848-19-4
First Edition 2018.

Copyright © James Aitchison 2018

The right of James Aitchison to be identified as the author of this work has been asserted by him in accordance with the Copyright, Designs and Patents Act of 1988.

All rights reserved.

Acknowledgements

Since the publication of *The Gates of Light* by Mica Press in 2016, new poems by James Aitchison have appeared in these and other journals:

Acumen, Brittle Star, The Frogmore Papers, The Herald, London Grip, The London Miscellany, New Writing Scotland, Painted,spoken, Poetry Salzburg Review, Reach Poetry, The Reader, The Recusant, Scottish Left Review, The Scottish Review, South.

In Memory of

Robert Nye (1939 - 2016)

Contents

In the Beginning	1
Telescope	2
Stargazing	3
The Seafarer Came This Way	4
Picture Hirta	5
On Iona	7
Soundings	7
On Cally Loch	7
On South Uist	8
On Barra in May	9
At Loch of Harray, Orkney	10
Gap Years	12
Possession	13
Good Morning, Face	14
Sharpening	15
Orders	15
Voices	15
Jurassic Genes	16
Cells	17
Smell	18
Their Fires Make Rain	19
Futures	20
Why Would a Wealthy Man …?	21
Love Stories	22
Behind the Waterfall	24
Holmes and I	27
Zoo Quest for Attenborough	28
Synchrotron	29
Stone Works	31
Our First Suicides	33
Duchy	34
Reckoning	35
The Years' Injustices	36
The Messiah in Tewkesbury Abbey	37
Severn, Avon, Forth	38
And the Pursuit of Happiness	40

Click on *Help*	41
Balancing	42
Staggering	42
Axe	43
Now	43
A Small Child	43
Learning How to Sing	44
Unknowing	46
Things I Know	46
Thanksgiving	47
Remember	47
End-plan	48
Cypress and Honeysuckle	49
Itinerary	50

IN THE BEGINNING

African Eve climbed down from her baobab tree.

We dig up skulls and carbon-date their age
but the capacity of a skull
can't tell us when our brain grew whorled enough
for Eve's tree to mutate into a *t r e e*.

By some genetic accident
our branching neural networks chanced on speech.
And so we say, 'In the beginning was the word.'

TELESCOPE
(Edwin Hubble: 1889-1953)

The black hole at the bottom of my mind
isn't wholly neurological.
It's bigger than the aphasic intervals
that always catch me in the act.

I found it, it found me a half-life past
before I'd heard of the astronomer,
Edwin Hubble and his telescope.

Hubble images on the tv screen
are like an orrery,
an idiot's guide to a universe I scan
in one encompassing glance.

And then I sense what the pictures never show:
billions of light-year gaps between the spheres.

My imagination ends where Hubble's begins:
his cosmic space is the black hole in my mind.

I can't make images of nothingness.
I live in fear of the unimaginable:
my whole mind might be sucked into the hole.

STARGAZING

Yeats, Jung, and Hughes practised astrology.
I've never seen star-creatures in the sky:
no Dog or Bull, Great Bear or Little Bear,
no Swan, no Pegasus and no Ploughshare.

I try again but my binoculars
and brass-bound telescope can't magnify
what's indiscernible to my naked eye.
Here in the cloudy north I can sit and stare
for hours before I see a single star.

But when I went outside at night to smoke
in an orchard in Up Hatherley
then I saw them. And the more I looked
the more I saw; not signs but stars that broke
cover and shone in spaces between stars:
angelic needlepoint, celestial joke
in spaces between spaces between stars.

THE SEAFARER CAME THIS WAY

I swayed to the rhythm of the tilting ship
as I stood smoking on the upper deck.

I felt it as a shower of rain at first,
the wind-whipped top-spray from the white-cap waves.
Sunlight and spindrift
cast shreds of pointillist rainbows in my face.

By oars, by mainsail, steering-board and stars
the Seafarer came this way
twelve centuries ago in an open boat.

The weather had changed when I went on deck that night:
Norse Voyager was steady, unwavering.

In June's long twilight
and the illusory light of a translucent moon
visibility was so clear
the perspective of *Norse Voyager's* wake –
a blue-green track with luminescent flecks –
narrowed so slowly it had no vanishing point.

PICTURE HIRTA

Hirta, less than five square miles in size, is the biggest of St Kilda's clustered islands, a group too small for most atlases and maps, too small to be called an archipelago.

One of the elders in the photograph taken on Hirta's cobbled single street looks like David Livingstone. Hirta was as far as Africa until the photographer arrived.

Spun wool, salted mutton and sheepskins, tweeds and shawls dyed lichen-crotal gold were bartered for roof timbers and steel-blade tools.

Tourists drawn by whims of hardihood came ashore in tailored clothes. Tourists had no goods for bartering; they paid cash. The islanders bought paraffin, tinned meat, chemical dyes and dreams of abundant worlds across the sea.

A ranger's wrist-hold steadied me for the steps from *MV Quest* to a zodiac, a rigid inflatable powered by Yamaha, to Hirta's quay.

In gift-shop greetings cards, illustrated histories and guides there were no photographs of the command, accommodation and storage blocks jerry-built by the Ministry of Defence and painted a shade of green too deep for Hirta's sparse grey grass.

There were no photographs of radar discs and antennae on the skyline of this westernmost Cold

War listening post; no photographs of the helicopter that can reach the Scottish mainland in an hour.

Young men migrated. Surnames disappeared from the register. Cousin married cousin. The gene pool shrank. No one tilled the soil. No one harvested crops of sea-birds' eggs from Hirta's cliffs. Turf roofs fell on floors of beaten earth.

The factor's house has been renovated and whitewashed for guardians of our natural heritage. 'Factor': a land agent who collected rents – on Hirta he collected rents-in-kind – for an absentee laird. Two lost cottages have been rebuilt for bird-ringers.

Dozens of cleits, dry-stone storage kilns like empty cairns, were whole; sheltered nestings for St Kilda wrens.

A wrist-hold steadied me onto the zodiac; another wrist-hold and I boarded *MV Quest*.

The last St Kildans were willing evacuees. They were transported to mainland farms, tubercular alleyways, vast skies, millennial forests and pasturelands.

The dark-fleeced, long-legged flocks of Soay sheep ran feral for years before the people left the land.

ON IONA

Walking across Iona, I passed by
the graves of Northern kings and queens who lie
with Celtic saints whose bones can't sanctify
my want of faith. I saw a skylark fly –
the brown bird dark against the daylight sky –
and watched until its song had flown so high
it was one of the floating nuclei
in the vitreous chamber of my eye.

We plough old meadows and sow wheat, oats and rye;
we spray our hunger on beetles, tares, fungi.
And each year for the loaves of bread we buy
ground-nesting breeding pairs of skylarks die.

SOUNDINGS

As intimate as the sounds of speech
are the conversations of the seas
around the Hebrides
and plainsong on a shingle beach.

ON CALLY LOCH

Beyond the golf course of the spa hotel
a mute swan sailing across the Cally loch
trails its silver wake into the reeds.
Only the wildest slice will reach its nest.

ON SOUTH UIST

In an instant
of split-second
time-lapse clarity
we saw it falling from the sky
a seeming-solid shawl of blue-grey cloud
the width of the windscreen
in the same instant
you braking
not veering
braking by reflex
faster than falling
faster too fast for fear
you and I bracing
brain-gut-and heart
for the thud
and the smear
in the next in the same
in the next instant
the cloud retracting its legs
folding its sinuous neck.

And then the little thrill of deliverance:
the windscreen was intact, and on wingbeats
slower than the beating of my heart
the blue-grey bird flew into blue-grey cloud.

ON BARRA IN MAY

I couldn't walk into the wind
made visible by flying sand.
I needed both feet on the ground
and even then I couldn't stand
upright against the wind; I leaned
on a hurricane of sound.

The west wind whummeled Barra's shore;
I tasted sea-salt on my tongue.
I stood, or stooped, for three or four
minutes with arms outstretched. I hung
my weight on that Atlantic roar
until my half-shut eyes were stung
to tears. I felt a vicious glee:
the Calmac ferry couldn't sail
in that May day's Atlantic gale.
Stormbound on Barra we were free.

AT LOCH OF HARRAY, ORKNEY

On the morning of the second day
the hotel was an island in the mist
and the loch was lost.

By noon the October sun was warm enough
to uncover the water
where mute swans browsed in separate families.

On Sunday morning gusts of wind and rain
thrashed ripples into breaking waves:
the scattered swans assembled near the shore.

Whooper swans would soon be coming south
from Iceland and Arctic Scandinavia
to the lesser winter of the Northern Isles.

The primordial sextant in a whooper's brain
is as sure as satnav.

★

Two offset crosses,
blue girdled by gold on a red ground –
I thought the hotel was flying the Norwegian flag.
'No,' the barman said. 'It's the Orkney flag.'

I should have known.
The flag is a twenty-first century design
but Orkney islanders were Norse for centuries.

Their new flag widens the gulf of the Pentland Firth;
the white St Andrew's cross on a blue ground
is the X of a foreign country.

I fly no flags.
I'm at ease here, where the North Sea
becomes migrating swans' Norwegian Sea.

★

At Ness of Brodgar, the isthmus
between Loch of Harray and Loch of Stenness,
a metropolis rises from our lost millennia.

GAP YEARS

Ernest Marples, Postmaster General
in the late 1950s,
sent hundreds of undergraduates and me
a letter of thanks for delivering Christmas mail.

In the '50s the words, 'a gap year', meant
you'd been sent down from university
or you'd had tuberculosis
and spent a year in a sanatorium.

My gap lasted decades before I saw
that the blessing I got from walking in the rain
made me oblivious
of my unpaid and now unpayable debt.

My ignorance is as inexcusable
as my excuse:
for three winters I went from street to street
and door to door delivering good news.

POSSESSION

Here in the north
there are more frost-bound days in a winter month
than there were in our five years in Gloucestershire,
and yet the garden is plentiful:
apples, raspberries, gooseberries and plums.

I say these things again
because each season seeds instinctual needs
and my brain sends pagan signals down my spine.

I work to repay my debts,
not to banks' money-laundering protection racketeers
but to gardens, gardening, the living dead and you.

I pay gladly
but I feel I haven't earned rights of ownership;
I hold the title deeds but no entitlement.
Possession brings a surreptitious glee.

Vote for a Party of the Dispossessed?
This is a small country but there is land enough.

I should plant more trees for the ones I've felled
in Stirlingshire and Gloucestershire
and the plantation I've pulped to poetry.

The seasons repeat their rhythms in my mind;
on a good day I slough twenty years.

A gargoyle squats on a staddle stone beside the pond.
A white hare crouches beneath a hazel tree.
The Green Man's head turns grey with weathering.

GOOD MORNING, FACE

I've grown light-headed from abandoning
opinions, principles, ideologies
and faith in the significance of dreams.

I'm free, I tell myself,
from mind-clogging encumbrances, and yet
I wake up with a grudge against the day.
I wake up with a grudge against waking up.

And that is why the shaving mirror says
'Good morning, face. Good face. Good morning, face.'

SHARPENING

When mind gives way and I need mindless chores
I sharpen loppers, shears and secateurs.

ORDERS

My brain has orders of reality
that come to mind in dreams and poetry.

My brain's a millennial litre-of-jelly space,
a sacred sacrificial slaughter-place.
My brain's in a dear life-long free fall from grace.

VOICES

Antibiotics and oxygen healed my lung.
My vocal cords, inflamed and swollen, clung
to my larynx, silencing my tongue.

An old man's voice may change if testosterone
falls and his pitch rises from baritone
or tenor to counter-tenor. I grunt. I groan.

JURASSIC GENES

I inherited its Jurassic genes.
They live in a prehistoric substrate of my brain.
The creature is invisible and real.

I felt it stir
when I saw vertically stitched skin
after open-heart surgery,
hysterectomy's stapled horizontal scar,
drainage tubes and a sac beneath a bed,
colour coded lines in a dance of life
and death across a bedside monitor.

Some patients must have known I was scared stiff.

A mind ago on days when I blacked out,
electrodes twitched in my fingertips,
bright selves were sucked through a vortex in my brain,
a dimmer-pad counted five-four-three-two-one
and the light went out.

Today these melodramas are black comedy.

The creature's weaker now.
It has claimed me only once in twenty years.
I know it's still alive, a natural force
and I know that nothing in the natural world,
not even abnormalities of mind,
can be unnatural.

CELLS

From methane to amoeba was our first.

We multiply. We divide. We recombine.

From amoeba's protozoan slime
to megalosaurus –

We died of gigantism and meteorites.

We mutate. We replicate. We mutate.

We died: we live in your children's picture books.
We live in your cinemas.
We live in your brain-stem's saurian cells.

We are plankton. We are basking sharks.

We are jellyfish. We pulsate in your warm seas.

We Neanderthals; we mapped the moon.
We are flint-knappers; we are mapping Mars.

We divide. We recombine. We multiply.

SMELL

From our first house to my first full-time job
I sometimes walked to work along farm roads.
In June the fields of broad beans blossoming
smelt like the kind of perfume a man could wear.

★

A neighbour gave me a bucket of pig's blood.
'Fertiliser. For your vegetables.'
I left the bucket in the greenhouse.

Two days later when I opened the door
the smell of butchery and sacrifice
bypassed my frontal lobes
and fired the reptile neurons in my brain.

★

When I was a lizard my breath was poisonous
and I could sniff out
the farthest whiff of putrefying flesh.

★

Thick brown-tipped matchsticks like Bengal lights
have cauterised both nostrils' nasal veins.
I cough and snotter small gobbets of congealed
blood
for two or three days and I lose all sense of smell.

THEIR FIRES MAKE RAIN

We draw up fossil layers through the earth's crust
and give them a second life by burning them.
We cremate our ransacked underworld
and give ourselves unearthly powers.

Plundering subterranean substances
and then incinerating them
seems unnatural in the natural world.

Our planet's atmospheres –
invisible gases made visible in clouds –
swell on thermals
from world-wide crematoria.

Our burnt-up fossils have another post-mortem life:
their fires make rain.

Noah's flood was ice-age meltwater.
The ice caps melt.

FUTURES

The land was fertile in their fathers' days:
commodity dealers in Paris and New York
brokered futures in coffee and sugarcane.

Earthquakes and aftershocks re-open fault-line chasms
that rise from earth's inchoate core.

Hurricane Daniel loosened the thin soil
on treeless slopes. Hills slid from hills
and swallowed hill-foot, tin-hut villages.

A tidal surge spread salt across the fields.

Voodoo is the peoples' litany
against cataclysm, typhoid and cholera.

The fertiliser on the fields is shit,
their own and that of chickens, goats and pigs.

WHY WOULD A WEALTHY MAN …?

Why would a wealthy man …?
We'd bought the servants' wing
of what had been an iron-master's house.

In the garden on the far side of the lawn
below a shallow covering of soil
my spade struck a foot-deep layer of foundry slag,
fused cinder-lumps, sharp-blistered, vitreous.

Why did he cover up this seam
when the great black landmark of the Cinder Hill,
spoil from his furnaces, was visible for miles?

I dug a waist-deep trench and re-buried the slag.

★

I sweat to let rough tasks last their full time
or as long as literate work allows.

In my unstable equilibrium
I have to learn again, again
that even piecemeal, interrupted tasks –
intransigent poems, vitreous cinder-lumps –
imprint their primitive ineradicable
alternating rhythms in my brain.

I'm a rich man, free to choose the kind
of tasks that grip my hands and fill my mind.

LOVE STORIES

Brain cells for falling in love do not exist
until you fall in love.
And then the new cells fire
in a swelling hallucinogenic flare
that dazzles other networks in your brain.

You know how it is:
can't eat, can't sleep, can't think of anyone but him.

Your mind's deranged by love until –
a year, a month, a week –
estrangement claims you and your love's deranged
by lovers' love-in-hate.

You could cut and run
or try to naturalise your statelessness.

Don't listen to this man.
He's lived so long his year is just a month
and a month for him is an autumn afternoon.

Your private quandary is everyman's,
or everywoman's in your case.
Remember who you were before you fell:
allow your overshadowed selves
back into an equalizing light.

Don't listen to this man.

Then there will be less fury in your love.
He and you will grow companionable:
you'll say the same word simultaneously
and finish one another's sentences.

Don't trust this man:
he's forgotten how it feels to fall in love.

You'll sleep safely in your love's curved shape,
and he in yours.

BEHIND THE WATERFALL

He hated his day job
unplanning and replanning planners' plans
for garages, conservatories, pigeon lofts.

He painted when Richard and Franny were asleep
and I lay waking for him to come to bed.
'I paint by moonlight,' he said, 'when the moon is full.'

Painters should live in cities or near the coast.

He kept his studio locked until – days, weeks
or even months – a painting was complete.

I loved his work. I've seen nothing of his for years.
I soon learned not to ask him where or how.
'Talent' was one of my earliest mistakes.
'It isn't talent,' he said. 'It's accomplishment.'

He said of one of his paintings
'It's the earth seen from a satellite in space
and so it's the earth in space.' Of another he said
'It's mosses and lichens on a boulderstone.'

I said something about shadows in one of his works.
'Yes. Can you see them lengthening and deepening?'

One of his paintings was layer upon layer
of different weathers in a day and night:
frost, mist, clouds, sunlight through falling rain
and strands of moonlight slanting through the dark.
'A view,' he said, 'from behind the waterfall.'

No, no, no, no. I make it sound as if …

No, not the work of a dabbling amateur.
That painting was beautiful,
abstract, factual, severely beautiful.

He needed women. He didn't need a wife.
He should have lived with childless mistresses.

★

Switzerland? The Tyrol? The Hebrides?

When anyone asked him where, he would say
'They're anywhere you like and nowhere you know.'

He took them when we split up. They were his, of course.

Some people felt – They didn't say 'bleak' or 'harsh'
but he knew what they meant, and he was pleased.

His landscapes were illusory and real,
remote, immediate, austerely beautiful.
Not light and darkness but what he called dark light.

Trees were skeletal and purple-black,
thin-streaked with snow and skewed by the west wind.
They vanished in rising mist or lowering cloud.

Vertical and diagonal drystone walls –
mould-blue, dove-grey and tipped with off-white snow –
climbed the foothills and faded stone by stone.

Clouds might have been mountains and mountains clouds.
Horizons were indiscernible;
I couldn't see where earth ended and sky began.

They were self-portraits, of course.

He said he'd burn them all. I'll never know.

HOLMES AND I

Watching an episode of *Sherlock Holmes*
one evening in a summer thunderstorm
I heard-and-saw the heart-leap two-in-one:
a crashing whump and a flash of cobalt blue
as lightning struck the rooftop aerial.

Holmes, played by Jeremy Brett, died instantly,
killed by darting particles of light
and an electronic sizzling hiss,
a blizzard of white noise on the tv screen.

Off! The remote. Switch off! And the set. Switch off!

When intervals between the speeds of sound
and light grew longer, I thought it safe enough
to switch the television on again.

Holmes was sitting in an armchair:
his eyes were closed, his lips curved in a smile
and on a table beside the chair – a pipe,
empty syringe and rubber ligature.

The problem's solved and the craving's satisfied.
I know these states of mind but I don't know how
Holmes and I survived the lightning strike.

ZOO QUEST FOR ATTENBOROUGH

When David Attenborough set out on his quest
for a dragon in the Komodo chain
of islands in southern Indonesia
in 1956, he didn't know
if the creature was zoological fact
or tribal lore. He had no photographs.

When the TV camera caught the beast,
a Komodo dragon, a lizard ten feet long,
and when the camera caught Attenborough
and the beast in the same frame, he didn't know
that if it had gone without carrion or prey
for a few days, it would scuttle-run
faster than a young zoologist.

★

Attenborough ages timelessly. He didn't grow old
until I saw his then and then his now,
from Attenborough the skinny nimble boy
following a python up a tree
to the ninety-year-old in interview.
And slower — half an octave lower? —
his voice-overs' disembodied voice.

★

That zoo quest for a dragon? If he had known
its bite was gangrenous
and its salivating mucous glands
were more haemophilic than warfarin,
he'd have kept talking to the lizard and me.

SYNCHROTRON

Billions of light-years, seven Biblical days
or instantaneously?
Physicists in their subterranean world
compute the origin of the universe.

★

I could be writing about final things.
I'm sitting on a third-floor balcony
watching big white-bellied Alpine swifts
feeding on air.

Inside a mountain in the Alps
physicists have built a synchrotron
to calculate the moment time began.

★

Even when I wear my training shoes
my feet and then my spine tell me I'm bored
with castles, cathedrals and Renaissance palaces.
I praise the scaffolders, stone masons and carpenters.

Flotillas of cormorants –
in Scotland I see them singly or in pairs –
are roosting on Lake Lugano in mid-afternoon.

Inside that hollow mountain in the Alps
subatomic particles
are programmed to collide at the speed of light.

★

Four young Asian women wearing high-heeled shoes
giggle in sisterhood
as they trundle their wheeled suitcases
uphill in Zermatt through the falling snow
that swallows the Matterhorn.

Inside the hollow mountain
physicists say the colliding particles
will echo the Big Bang, without the bang.

★

My first sure sighting of a great-crested grebe
was on one of the lochaned moonscape Uist Isles
where peopled crofts are lost
in hectares of uncultivable land.

Full-fed after a morning's foraging
on water beetles, larvae and minnow-size fish
a flock of great-crested grebes
drowse on the water a few metres away
from lunch-time strollers and family picnickers
on the shore of Lake Como.

★

The power that scatters suns and galaxies
in an expanding universe
will wipe our planet from its firmament.

My mind's last faculty
is the mystery of a simpleton:
I praise scaffolders, stone masons and carpenters;
I celebrate swifts, cormorants and grebes.

STONE WORKS

Checking the *i* and *y* in *Sisyphus*
I found a word for a recurring state of mind:
sisyphism – performing useless tasks,
sweaty physical or mental work
that has no purpose but the penitence
of sweaty physical or mental work.

Sandstone

My first wall was of sandstone, double-width,
mortared between each width and block by block.

The work lasted for months.
My hands were too calloused for poetry.

Topped with coping, the wall stood four feet high.
Some stones metamorphosed into words.

Drystone

A long, low gently curving drystone wall
carved sloping ground into two terraces:
a vegetable garden and a level lawn.

Making-unmaking-remaking – selecting stones
was slow and aching-sweet as poetry.

Boulderstone

Hundreds of ill-matched half-sunk boulderstones
made rigid, zigzag, criss-cross, dead-end paths.

The boulders had been carried to the Carse
and rounded smooth by the same glacier
but every stone

had a variegated colour, size and shape.

I loosened the stones and re-positioned them
like the first contour lines on a new map
or the intonation contours of a poem.

Whinstone

The local soil is clay but around the house
I found mounds, rows, single chunks of whin,
oddly angled, sharp-edged igneous stones
too multifaceted for building blocks.
And yet … A whim …

By counterpoising rocks' unevenness
whin and I built another drystone wall.

Stone Works

Stone works are older than poetry:
they keep my first illiterate self alive.

OUR FIRST SUICIDES

'Often, very often, Sylvia and I would talk at length about our first suicides […] We talked death and this was life for us'.
Anne Sexton: 'The Bar Fly Ought to Sing' in *No Evil Star*

Thrilled by the rhythms of each other's voice
reading poems in Lowell's seminar,
Anne and Sylvia drove to the Boston Ritz,
drank martinis
and gossiped suicidal rhapsodies.

A high-pitched glee of poetry and gin
tipped the balance of their polarities
to manic sisterhood:
suicide would deliver them from death
and from the personal familial myth
of a priapic father-god.

They didn't say 'attempts at suicide':
they spoke as agents of the living dead.
Each new poem would be posthumous.

Anne looked in the bathroom mirror: her lips were worms.
She looked again: she was a rat.
She sat in her parked car. Nowhere to go.
She coupled a snaking hosepipe to the exhaust,
looked in the driving mirror and mouthed goodbye.

Young Esther was an American fantasist.
This was England: unholy matrimony,
insufferable single parenthood.
Sylvia knelt down in the English way
and turned the little brass knob.
The escaping sigh was barely audible.

DUCHY
(Edward Kennedy 'Duke' Ellington: 1899-1974)

Green's Playhouse, Glasgow
was a northern outpost on his farewell tour.

Ellington and the elders in his band –
Hodges, Bigard, Williams, Carney, Brown –
came from cotton fields to the Cotton Club
where white folk danced to a black composer's tunes.

I entered his duchy to hear the Duke hold court.

The players on the Playhouse stage that night
looked older than the men in the photographs.
On the road for more than thirty years
they had grown white-haired, arthritic, venerable.

'Solitude', 'Take the A Train', 'Caravan' –
the big band played symphonic black-man blues.

Ellington rose from his piano stool.
Centre-stage, a silent soloist
in rhythm with the double bass and drums,
he bounced invisible tennis balls –
one, two, one-two-three-four –
and lobbed them over the invisible net
to detonate among the audience.

His farewell tour
was a world-wide caravan of one-night stands.
The A Train halted at Woodlands Cemetery.

I'm almost deaf but the cortex is intact:
I hear the ghost train on its farewell tour.

RECKONING
(i. m. Douglas Kilpatrick)

To know some of the ways of waves and air
you built a boat and learned to sail, steer, tack
against, aslant and with whatever wind
blew across the lochs of Galloway.

Your hesitations when we met to talk –
I see it now – were natural time-lapses.
You were reckoning from first principles
and wondering how long the game would last.

To make sound sense of melody and rhythm
and to be versed in music's wordlessness
and smell absinthe on Django Reinhardt's breath
you made a guitar and taught yourself the chords.

You left it late but you made time to learn
the liberating discipline of paint.
Your hills and shorelines make a masterly
all-weather map of shadowland and light.

THE YEARS' INJUSTICES
(i. m. Douglas Middleton)

In a newsroom of jangling telephones
and chattering manual typewriters
he worked unhurriedly,
editing dozens of stories in an eight-hour shift.

He looked and sounded ten years older than I
when we first met in 1966.

He was in command:
his jurisdiction was Edinburgh,
the towns and villages of the Lothians,
West Fife, Roxburgh, Selkirk, Peebleshire
and the trust of two hundred thousand readers a day.

Twenty-five years later we worked side by side
practising the complicated craft
of simple prose,
knowing there can be no mastery.

Eye-to-eye, he and I were the same height,
but even then …
And in the twenty years since then
he grew taller, more substantial,
larger in absence than in life.

His obituary gave his age as seventy-one,
five years younger than I was on the day.
And in the photograph
he wore the pure white beard of a wise old man.

I've grown fat on the years' injustices.

THE MESSIAH IN TEWKESBURY ABBEY

I heard the pulse of an echo in the long last chord
of the orchestra and choristers.
And then that echo of a posthumous life
was cut short by the applause of an audience
released from the discipline of listening
to the ascension of Christ in Tewkesbury.

The diminuendo echo of the praise
ended, and they began to chat their way
towards mincemeat pies and alcohol-free mulled wine
on trestle tables in the west aisle of the nave.

I went outside. The night air was so still
I lit my pipe first time. I know. I know.
And I know that an old man with tinnitus
in his deaf right ear and half-hearing in his left
can tune his hearing aid
to the pitch of an imperceptible frequency.

When I went in again
people were chattering louder to be heard
chattering above their chattering.
In the noise of voices
I couldn't make out a word of human speech.

And then I heard –
too high above the din for others to hear –
the ghosts of choristers
in dark corners of the ceiling's barrel vaults
breathing, whispering
the chorus of a lost oratorio.

SEVERN, AVON, FORTH

We were living in Cheltenham in the summer of the flood.

Severn and Avon
and all their swollen tributaries
and new headwaters streaming down country roads
converged on Cheltenham and Tewkesbury.

Drains overflowed
and the conjoint force of sewage and rainwater
thrust iron manhole covers into the air.
A mixture of fresh rain and human waste
surged through the streets.

Tewkesbury Abbey was an island in a brown sea.

Pollution entered the filtration plant at Mythe:
water mains were shut down for two weeks.

(Do not trust this man.
He showered in water from a private reservoir.)

Millions of bottles of free takeaways
of Holywell Malvern Water and Highland Spring
were stacked in carparks throughout Gloucestershire.

The flood was a 'once-in-a hundred-years-or-more'
and centuries of man-made atmospheres.

(You must not trust this man.
His house in Cheltenham
was at the end of a private cul-de-sac
on the ridge between the racecourse and the town.
He escaped scot-free and went back to Stirlingshire.)

Our house on the Stirling Carse
is fifty yards away from the River Forth.
We're miles inland but the River is tidal here.

AND THE PURSUIT OF HAPPINESS

The unfastening of frontal consciousness
might be a circumstance,
and if happiness is this half-mind faculty
then it cannot be pursued.

Once it was music,
not music in the mind
but mind's metamorphosis in music's metaphors:
moon-pull tides and thermals of angels' breath.

Now it might follow the end of seasonal tasks,
repetitive, rhythmic practicalities
of wordless garden work.

And even before a task's complete
I sometimes overhear my illiterate brain
in a preternatural buoyancy
celebrate my mind's oblivion
in the hydrophonic yawning song of whales,
the hum of obedient bees in foxglove bells,
the snuffle-grunt of a truffle-hunting pig.

I make no explicit wish for happiness:
it happens, or not, only afterwards
when I get my mind back whole or nearly whole.

CLICK ON *HELP*

New generations of multi-media tools
are engineering their designers' minds.
New software programs have new protocols;
my ageing neurons must be re-aligned.

And so I try again. No joy. I try
again. I start to sweat. Again. Nonsense.
I feel I'm being interrogated by
a man-made alien intelligence.

I check the section in the user's guide:
incomprehensible. The words don't fit
my brain's language centres, codified
so long ago they mutter 'Shite!' not 'Shit!'

If I'm to follow the designer's train
of thought I must adjust my contour lines.
I click on *Help*. Helpless, because my brain's
capacity is less than the machine's.

BALANCING

When I bend down and straighten up too soon
the floor tilts and the walls lean out of line
and bloodrush fireflies flicker in my eyes.

The plastic skin of the pump-up doll, my muse,
has brittled with abuse and age: she's cracked.

In my tinnient deaf right ear I hear
another span of scaffolding collapse.

Another year, and I'm more or less the same.
I'm more. I'm less.
I've more than I need but much less than I want.

Dressing and undressing
I fail the 'Can-you-stand-on-one-leg?' test.

I practise balancing but I still fall down.

STAGGERING

In February when I finally dug out
the last of the wooden railway sleepers –
planted as borders, side-on, two-thirds deep –
I staggered in a sweet delirium
of sweat and creosote.

AXE

My new hand-axe is shaped like the first axe
but now it's a single casting, blade and shaft,
that grips the iron-age neurons in my brain.

NOW

An hour of longing is life-long for him,
the bored child caged in Now's great interim.
An infant sleeps among the cherubim.

A SMALL CHILD

A small child hears snakes hiss
in her parents' whisperings

learns the first of guilt
in her parents' undertones

is abandoned by her parents' silences

fears snakes
when her mother switches off the light

is unborn in her parents' absences

knows that the meanings in her parents' speech
mean more than the meanings of spoken words

may be loved and yet feel desolate

LEARNING HOW TO SING

At birth an astrophysicist's neural cells
are the same as a poet's, but when their fontanelles
enclose their skulls, their brains diverge and swell
until through puberty, chance, science and art
their minds are galaxies apart.

★

Trapping spoken words in an alphabet
was once as daft
a notion as catching water in a net.

I'm an apprentice endlessly in debt
to the art and craft:
when words fail me or I fail words I sweat.

You never learned and so you can't forget.
Your doodle-draft
is artless but it's craftily typeset.

★

Through 'revision and slogwork', Heaney said,
a poem can gather spontaneity.
He wrote in the tonal contours, tenor pitch
and rhythms of premeditated speech.

He knew that feeling-into-thought occurred
minutes, months before the written word.
And knew the labouring that might lie ahead
of a natural delivery.

★

Not knowing how or why, I search again
my miniaturised measureless domain –
the loose-leaf lexicon in my brain.

I grunted, groaned, found I was found by words
that verbalise my vocal cords
and peck my inner ear like twittering birds.

Language shaped my palate, teeth, tongue, lips.
It gave me alphabetic fingertips
and email attachment paperclips.

★

I'll carry on until the neural sluice
runs dry and dying networks cry, 'A truce?'

I'll send my work to editors half my age
in places I'd never think of visiting.

I'm still in debt, still paying the mortgage,
still learning how to sing.

UNKNOWING

In my unknowing
I sometimes think that what I think are thoughts
are pensioned fantasies:
imagination, memory and dreams
are time-free zones;
mystery is an intrinsic faculty
and sacred places in the physical world
are sanctified in places of my mind.
I pilfer miracles.

THINGS I KNOW

'Write about the things you know.'
I can't know if these lines will grow
to poetry, for a poem is true
only when at last I find
what's hidden in my substrate mind:
things I didn't know I knew.

THANKSGIVING

'I find it easier to write than not.'
Yesterday's words sound like hubris now
but they were a thanksgiving, not a boast,
the words of a near-innumerate old man
trying but losing
count of an astonishment of stars.

REMEMBER

You and I remember different things
and the same things differently.
Together we recall all we need to know.

We tend a rose garden:
I spray for mildew, greenfly and blackspot;
you prune hard for the next blossoming.

END-PLAN

Short, zig-zag, criss-cross-purpose dead-end paths;
hard-standing slabbed with concrete three-by-twos;
three circular flower beds in the lawn –
We eliminated the geometry.

Rhododendrons' contorted trunks;
viburnum branches fused with hawthorn;
a rambling bramble-barred entanglement –

We pruned hard. I felled sprawling elder trees
and ripped out snowberries' long white lateral roots.

We had no end-plan:
this loose-leaf landscaped informality
was created as much by chance as by design.

Ten years, and on three or four days a year
when a task grows onerous
the garden's simplicity looks unnatural –
I should have spared the snowberries –
and its re-ordering so obvious
I fear it may have nothing new to say.

A groundless fear, of course:
a garden grows more surely than poetry.

CYPRESS AND HONEYSUCKLE

Their shadows grew deeper and heavier year by year.
To let light and air
into the dark corner of the garden
I cut off the dull green branches and crowns
of twin cypress trees.

Lopped cypresses don't generate new growth.

Two more trees, not felled this time
but reduced to a pair of columns of brown bark.
Non-native but even so
I felt uneasy. Not guilty but exposed.

Last year was it…? Two years ago…? Or three…?
I have a closing-down-sale sense of time.
You planted a rooted stem of honeysuckle
in the thin soil between the two bare trunks.

Honeysuckle? The name and that small root
seemed too tender for the climate on the Carse.

Now dozens of purple tendrils bind the trunks
lost beneath the simple soft green leaves.
And on some tendrils' tips
flowers' red sepals are two tiny cupped hands
with their fingers apart.
Creamy-white stigmas, styles and filaments
emerge from yellow petals' open curves.
Berries are ripening from red to black.

And the tendrils are growing longer day by day;
feelers are swaying for more light and air.

ITINERARY

We seldom booked ahead; we just set off
sure we'd find a room before nightfall.

> Are lorries still trailing clouds of quarry dust
> along Wenlock Edge?

You noted road numbers and names on the AA map,
four miles to an inch, and planned our route.

> Does the Hailes Church flock still pray by candlelight?

> The gun-butts on the Long Mynd were overgrown
> with gorse and dog-rose.

You drive and roadside place names match the sketch
of the itinerary printed in your mind.

> Dippers were bob-bob-bobbing in the beck –
> 'We just call it the beck' – at Mary Mount.

We sometimes missed a turning on first-time roads
and had to guess at a detour or check the map
or circle twice around a roundabout.

> In Up Hatherley by Cheltenham
> we made an orchard from a small farm's refuse tip.

> Midweek, off-season on a rainy afternoon
> we walked alone around Balcary Bay.

'Road Closed'. We couldn't find diversion signs
and lost our whereabouts for two or three hours
until we saw a roadside name we knew.

We may not know exactly where we are
but we know where we want to be at the end of the day.

Year after year you find our way from here
to there and back again to the right house.

Notes

Page 3, Stargazing

Letters on Poetry from W. B. Yeats to Dorothy Wellesley (Oxford and New York, 1964) 15 November, 1935: 'My wife and I looked at your horoscope last night.'

The Freud/Jung Letters (London, 1979)
Jung to Freud 8 May 1911: 'At the moment I am looking into astrology, which seems indispensable for a proper study of mythology.'
Jung to Freud 12 June 1911: 'My evenings are taken up very largely with astrology.'

Sylvia Plath: Letters Home – Correspondence 1950-1963 (London 1976)
July 5, 1958: 'We did our Ouija board for the first time in America.'
December 24, 1960: 'Ted is going to work out horoscopes.'

Biography

James Aitchison was born in Stirlingshire in 1938 and educated at Glasgow and Strathclyde Universities. In the 1960s he worked as a publicity copywriter at The Scotsman Publications in Edinburgh, after which he held a series of minor posts in Scottish colleges and universities. He and his wife lived in Gloucestershire for five years and returned to Stirlingshire in 2007. James Aitchison is a former poetry critic at *The Scotsman* and *The (Glasgow) Herald*.

What the critics wrote:

The Gates of Light (Mica Press, 2016)

'At the heart of it are a sustained sense of wonder and humility in the face of the created world, and a wary thankfulness that the powers are still there to chart the tiny and major changes of the seasons. […] Mica Press is to be thanked for the excellent job in putting together a collection as important as this by one of the most enduring and significant poets.'
Peter Carpenter, *The North*

'The arrival of *The Gates of Light*, Aitchison's first collection since 2009 is a cause for celebration. […] The collection's title *The Gates of Light* manages to combine the central themes of the book perfectly: the threshold between life and death, the material gates and the intangible light.
Richie McCaffery, *London Grip*

'He celebrates many of nature's enduring qualities, both in the wild and in the cultivated spaces of gardens. In several of the very fine poems in this collection, he shifts from the human perspective to the cosmic, and shows how entwined they are. […] James Aitchison takes concepts of apparent simplicity, but in the expression of personal experience we find a universality that we can relate to […] This collection was a pleasure to read. The poems shift through seasons and the vast elements of sea, land and air, with particular reference to the birds that move with apparent ease from one to the other; and all of us, trees, birds, humans and planet affected by that great star that sheds the light that permeates these poems.'
Morelle Smith, *The Scottish Review*

'His perspective allows a generous encompassing vision with a sharp awareness of the beauty and horror of the world, and a deeply moving acceptance of the probable closeness of death'.
Maggie Butt, *Acumen*

'The poet looks back across his whole life and shares often searing memories and observations.'
Charlotte Gann, *The Frogmore Papers*

Foraging: New and Selected Poems (Worple Press 2009)

"The measure is driven by natural speech cadence and yet it is artful, emotive and memorable. It takes a lifetime of reflective practice to write as simply as that. It is a joy to read. James Aitchison has grace and charm and a beauty of form and feeling."

Helena Nelson, *The Dark Horse*

"The natural world in its many manifestations has been a consistent theme down the years, but Aitchison is also willing to map more private and personal territory, and does this quite disarmingly. […] A very satisfying collection."

Jeremy Page, *The Frogmore Papers*

Other works by James Aitchison:

Poetry ~

Brain Scans (Scottish Cultural Press 1998)
Second Nature (Aberdeen University Press 1990)
Spheres (Chatto & Windus 1975)
Sounds Before Sleep (Chatto & Windus 1971)

(Critics who praised the above included Donny O'Rourke, Robert Nye, Edna Longley and Elizabeth Jennings.)

Critical Studies ~

New Guide to Poetry and Poetics (Rodopi Editions, 2013)
The Golden Harvester: the Vision of Edwin Muir (Aberdeen University Press 1988)

Edited ~

New Writing Scotland (Association for Scottish Literary Studies) with Alexander Scott. Volumes 1, 2, 3 (1983, 1984, 1985)

Textbooks ~

The Cassell Guide to Written English (Cassell 1994)
The Cassell Dictionary of English Grammar (Cassell 1996).

www.ingramcontent.com/pod-product-compliance
Lightning Source LLC
Chambersburg PA
CBHW042121100526
44587CB00025B/4140